L.I.F.E. Is A-MAZE-ING: CHRONICLES OF KALIYM FOSTER

L.I.F.E. Is A-Maze-ing: Chronicles Of Kaliym Foster

ISBN: 978-0-557-67685-9

Table of Contents

"Life has no table of contents…

There is no order…

The recipe varies…

Its contents are unknown…

U have to go through it to know its ingredients…

Information is the nutrients

Lack of knowledge is a horrible diet

It is the cause of a person becoming narrow-minded"

"You can predict…

but you actually don't know what you are going to get"

THE INTRODUCTION: POINT OF CONCEPTION

Beyond this point consists of a book of poetic short stories that are actual life experiences at a level you have never heard before.

The contents of this book are far beyond true.

When you read this book it will seem like day-sha-voo.

In reality, one or all of these experiences may have happened to you.

If these experiences have not happened to you in the near future they will happen to you.

What your mind is about to encounter will leave you intrigued.

This is a book about life that does not take a lifetime to read.

L.I.F.E is **LEARNING INFORMATION FROM EXISTENCE**.

You would have to exist first before you begin to experience.

If you are not en**light**ened then you will not be able to see certain aspects within our reality.

Life cannot exist without **L.I.T.E. (Learning Information Through Experience)**

L.I.T.E. serves as guidance to our sight.

You would have to at first go through it **(L.I.T.E.),**

before you learn from it **(L.I.F.E.) Learning Information From Experience**

Knowledge blossoms in the brain and allows the mind to grow.

If there is not anything you know: then your mind is still in a stage known as an embryo.

WISDOM IS THE KEY!!!

L.I.F.E. Is A-Maze-Ing

L.I.F.E. IS A-MAZE-ING L.I.F.E.; Learning Information From Existence
It is a complex topic with an endless sentence.
It requires an exclusive use of the senses.
U will see things in many tenses.
If u take L.I.F.E. serious,
then L.I.F.E. can become Learning Information From Experience.
What this means is to get your hands dirty and to become curious.
Some situations can make us smile.
Some situations may make us furious.
For some of us this path may last a while.
For some of us this path may not last a mile.
L.I.F.E. is a maze with a patterned lifestyle.
L.I.F.E. is a maze.
There are numerous approaches amongst many ways.
For every path there lies a discovery.
Through all the things you encounter you must conclude L.I.F.E. in summaries.
That is the part that becomes puzzling.
L.I.F.E. is a maze.
Some events can be inspirational leaving us amazed.
L.I.F.E. has value.
You are the one who determines the cost and how it becomes appraised.
L-I-F-E- that is L.I.F.E.'s monograms.
Its definition has more depth than the shallow word itself, one must actually live to understand.
L.I.F.E. has many holograms.
Some scenes can be seen and unseen by an average man.
There are times where a hologram can contradict the projection of its program.
For some, the contents of this hologram
creates an image within the skull of man.
We then begin to view things unlike others can.
These visions are epic thoughts within the dimensions of a brain.
These visions adjust the contrast of one's mind frame.
For the unprepared brain, these visions will drive them insane.

L.I.F.E. IS A-MAZE-ING

This is a consequence for jumping into the fast lane.

They JUMP because their hearts are untamed.

Emotions can spark pain if these emotions are not contained.

L.I.F.E. is a maze.

There are many waypoints within one point.

Every point has purpose and a point.

In some instances, these are awkward positions in which you will be appointed.

These positions can lead you to excitement.

Other positions can lead you to become disappointed.

L.I.F.E. is a maze.

It can keep u guessing.

It teaches u lessons... with a language called charades.

It is up to you to solely guess the phrase.

L.I.F.E. is A-MAZE-ING.

It's a puzzle that can become mentally engaging.

Your outlook will be forever changing as life becomes L.I.F.E. through a process called aging.

Some of us can go through this process called aging and still don't apply a single formula to an equation.

L.I.F.E. is truly A-MAZE-ING....

L.I.F.E. (Learning Information From Experiences)

I never thought I would be a cop

I once was a part of the resistance committing crime when the sun drops

Now I am in a position with a power to arrest transporting offenders to jails in which they would be housed in cell blocks

They say breaking an oath is a form of being crooked

I never see why we arrest people who use rocks

The solution for them should be an indefinite detox

Being that I was on the force for so long my mind began to see plots

When an officer does wrong he will be placed in the same place a criminal belongs

There is no particular side we are on

We are just enforcing a government's plan; laws that are not our own

As an officer the government didn't *give* us this power

This is power *we loan*

Once we are off the force we are like citizens powerless and on our own

Being employed as a cop is just a role play and this uniform is just a prop

Like a robot I am programmed to say Freeze!!! Stop!!!

How will I defeat that mental program when I turn in my gun and my badge drops?

Is there such a thing as a good or bad cop???

Well as for me I think not

Today a guy got shot and it was from my government issued glock

The hollow points made his heart stop

THE OATH

It was because he was parked in a handi-capped spot while he was observing a guy making a large deposit in a bank drop

I was patrolling on night watch assuming the duty of a night cop I heard a loud pop

To protect that citizen's life I fired a gunshot

The perp's shirt was covered with blood spots

He bled then eventually his corpse drops

As for me, I never believed in probability or people who had the ability to tell the future with heightened psychic ability

I was always told that angels are around me and that going through life will make u become psychic

As I age in which I refer to age as a number that is a measurement of degree

I began to see why they call it "**A Circle Of Life**"

L.I.F.E. is geometry; like at age 30 u see things at a certain degree

that would make me 30 degrees

If u were age 20 u would not see things from the same aspect and angle as me unless u began to participate in the circle of life's circumference through experience and responsibility

Maybe that's the definition of the holy trinity; three's company

It depends on who u are that influences the angle of view that p-o-v-(point of view) is what can become of thee

I arrested many criminals as an officer with handcuffs I place on their wrists under lock and key

The district attorney writes an indictment dependent upon the evidence they see

The judge may not see what we see to give that criminal guilty verdict or plea

The law enforcement tree is just like a branch or leaf on a tree

If the root of trees was in conflict of interest with its branch or stem or leaves all growth will then stop die and freeze

This is the introduction; the birth of corruption

If a system has no junction that is a system that will cease to function

One day I arrested a drunken

That drunken guy was going to some sort of celebration function

THE OATH

At that celebration function there was going to be a bomb that erupted causing a mass destruction

His life would not have been a presumption

This is a primary example to all people

To which power is not just in the hands of the badge or the United States; nor the symbol of stars stripes and an eagle

Power extends beyond the authorities; it is beyond: legal citizens, law-enforcement, and other common people

We are constantly put in situations in which we must choose good or the lesser of two evils or both could exist equal/unequal

Giving a citation to a poor family in a financial situation or letting go of that situation in favor of that person's gratification

What if that person hurts another person and causes a homicide investigation?

Choice never runs smooth like an angelic voice

I was given the power to write a ticket instead I didn't write that ticket because his scheduled court date was the same date he was scheduled to get evicted

I didn't appear to court in order to cause them to dismiss that ticket

The man then had the necessary monies to pay that landlord so he would not get evicted

If I didn't write that ticket he would have continued to speed in excess of the speed that is restricted

A second too fast could have ended in a situation that is horrific

It is funny how if I didn't stop him in a matter of minutes he would have gone to his apartment complex and shot up all the tenants

This would have resulted in him being a felony defendant

He was under the influence of alcoholic liquids

By me stopping him for a total of 55 minutes because my computer system was down malfunctioning because of glitches this was enough time to allow the gentleman to sober up and come to his senses

If I didn't make that stop and continued to mind my business it could have been a matter of death or stitches

Being employed with the law allowed me to see something called control of universal law

THE OATH

I think they call it probable cause because there is a high probability universal laws can affect these other things if they become involved

Everything cannot be single-handedly resolved

When I say we I mean we as in everyone must get involved

If one thing whether it be an action or function comes to a pause u may then never know what the consequence of the lack of responsibility may cause

An oath is not just limited to people who protect and serve

An oath is living by and up to your word

When life teaches u a lesson and that lesson is heard then the partaking in responsibility of those particular events must be served

Life makes u psychic through repetition

Life is an academy of repetition

Repetition creates prediction of events based upon what u have seen in the past or present tense

These experiences lead to premonitions

U can now predict people's actions and intentions

Role Play

(L.I.F.E. is but a stage act)…

Characters of the same book just a different stage;

This is a phrase that will become more understood as we age

My mother passed before I reached my infant phase

My memory of her is vague

"I am a soul that is brave" throughout my life I constantly heard that phrase

from people included in the many environments in which I was raised

The meaning of a name is valuable it can be appraised

These were the words requested to be engraved throughout my mother's will on my forearm before my mother was placed in her grave...

I was told the last words she said before she died on her hospitalized bed:

"L.I.F.E. is a maze, nothing is impossible u must discover, find, and make a way

I was given a vision of this child's destiny during his embryo stage

And this child's mission is a special mission

His mission is to save and pave a way for those whose minds are encaged"

ROLE PLAY

It has now been 3 decades

I always had a tendency to attract an audience of people whose minds are compact

I don't understand that

In fact, I always was unwilling to interact with people whose minds are compact

I ask myself:

What do these people lack..?

Why is it when these particular groups of people have difficulties I am the one they wish to contact..?

These people have gone to every psychologist and every psychiatrist and their problems still exist

I don't understand this: why am I the one called upon to assist these people whose minds are caught in an abyss

People say I must make a reality of mother's so called myth

Her myth was she believed I had a gift

I wanted to research this so I went to the archives; a place that holds records of countless lives

I searched through my file and found a bunch of lies

My name appears to have been changed when my father married his second bride

I asked myself:

Why is this information he desires to hide...?

For a moment I was in a temporary state of denial,

until I proofread my file

My name is Angel Abby Gates

Not Archie Angel Gray

Wait!!! This had to be a mistake

I discovered something else written on these paper slates

As my subconscious mind awakes it seems as if my father was not of the United States...

ROLE PLAY

He was of the United Arab Emirates

He had two mates

My mother Angel Gates

and his wife Abby Grey

According to the sources they both were his soul mates

I guess he concealed this information so I will never discover my fate

His name printed on this certificate of birth which I discovered is fake is Justin Gates

According to the security guards logs he visited the archives under another name that is false

Angel Walls...???

in an attempt to destroy records so my truths will be lost...

Hmmm two wives... In the United States u can't be a polygamist

I wonder is he still alive...?

Where is his current residence...?

Pondering as I gradually clench my fists

I am now in my 3rd decade

I am still attracting an audience of people who are deranged and crazed

People seem to love the music and the lyrics I compose and play

Some say, my sound and my voice grasps immediate attention

I possess an incredible ability through lyrics to make a dark mind turn day

Outside of my music phase I possess the same light

It seems not to fade into the shade

The same character I portray to make a dark mind turn day seemed to remain at bay

This talent is still present when my limelight fades...Wow!!

Who am I ...?

ROLE PLAY

I ask as I am stuck in a daydream dazed...

For three consistent decades I have made miracles and made it through miracles

Through the simple utterance of words I have converted altheas into the spiritual

My talent is not gossip

I have made people who seem psychotic logical all just with a simple application of guidance and dedication

I have made the minds of the unconscious to conscious with guidance

I am their compass

I naturally possess skills of people who has years of college

I seem to have an underlying talent to make the deep become shallow and the complex simple

Through my methods of knowledge I know now why I am the person people wish to encompass

I am now in the ending point of my 3rd decade

After years of continuous searching I finally found my father with the help of his bride's maid

I stood before him and asked a series of questions

He replied with intense emotion and little affection

I asked him: *why did u try to conceal my identity...?*

He replied pitifully: *I am afraid of u...?*

U possess an ability to change what seems unchangeable, to make the complex un-complex, and u do these tasks with simplicity

So I attempted to manipulate the legal records so u wouldn't detect the difference between u and me..?

I guess your birth was a message from god and this message must be encrypted

I said to him: *what difference*

He replied*: distance*

I said to him (*confused): distance...????*

He said*: yes I am altheas and I don't believe god exists*

Through your actions the image of an angel is what u depict

ROLE PLAY

Sorry I have denied your existence... I guess I was blessed with an angel; my own infant

U see an angel is not just a person with a halo who drifts in the skies with the wings in which he is uplifted

An angel is a person who can talk like us, eat like us, he or she is just extra-ordinarily gifted..in these select areas they can be highly intelligent

I said to him: *your attitude seems quite rigid why are u so frigid???...*

He then handed me some documents and told me to pay attention to the highlighted areas listed...

ROLE PLAY

Archie- derives from the word arch meaning a bridge

Angel- a demi-god or supernatural being

Abby- name derives from the word abyss; abyss as in lost or void

Gray -a gray area an impartial zone balanced an area that displays great humility and humbleness

Angelica Gates- was your mother angelica derives from the word angelical meaning angel like; supernatural

Gates-meaning a fence; passage way

Angelica Gates gave birth to and made a passage way to a path to another angel.. my son Angel

She says she seen at the time of conception a vision a child will be born a special child

Abby Gray- served as the color gray by remaining in a gray area which is borderline area by taking care of a child that was not hers being that she was not the birth mother...with mental stability the child Angel Abby Gates began inheriting gray area like qualities by always remaining balances mentally and physically.. I changed the name of my son Angel Abby Gates to Archie Abby Gray and he immediately within his early adulthood life began serving as an arch; a bridge a gateway by helping others leading them from the void by making a way for them to escape surroundings, mental states, and environments that seemed impossible to escape from.. He directed people out of these complex and difficult situations known as a MAZE...

After reading all the details and how it relates

I knew my father knew of my destiny and my fate..

O my god!!!

I am a semi-god

To be continued....

Role Play 2:

I thought I was so sure of myself but now I am confused

What I have discovered shocked me it blew my fuse

Surrounded in a realm of darkness like a man on the moon

I sit and pray in this dim lit room

with my first and second hand joining one another like a clock that reads twelve noon

I pray because I am eager to dispose of this melancholy mood

God can be fair and forgiving and on the flipside ruthless and shrewd

My faith in him I shall not lose

If I continue to brood and discontinue to move forward and dispose of this melancholy mood

I will be moving backwards

Moving backwards sparks old mood

If u move backwards M-O-O-D will spell D-O-O-M

It is quite a coincidence how emotions that are past tense

will lead to a destiny of destruction in your future tense

The truth hurts

No, I meant the truth mega hurts

I cry out loud to god in a loud uncontrollable burst

I wonder can he hear the mega hertz?

Did he receive my frequency?

Am I in tune with thee?

I should know that I am in tune

I once resided in the heavens now I am a guardian angel on earth to these earthly goons

By the desires of this world I was consumed

Money, clothes, cars, jewelry, sex,

I once admired the simple things in life but living gave birth to desire

ROLE PLAY 2

Desire made my influences complex

My desires would seem to never end I would just move to the next to the next to the next

Next!!!

I am an angel embodied in this flesh

I am guilty because I know I am not living at my very best

On my judgment day I wonder can I plea no contest

I got caught up in moving too fast in the fast lane of this fast life

On judgment day during my after L.I.F.E. can I plea nolo

to prevent me from paying for my first class ticket to hell to meet the man below

I then exited this dim-lit room in a state of mind where I began to assume

I thought since everything was handed to me with a silver spoon

to the harsh realities of this sick world I was immune

I realized swiftly my train of thought was an illusion like a cartoon

I was once an angel in the heavens with wings like a butterfly out the bloom

Now, I am a student like everyone else in this pupil stage trapped in this cocoon

The cocoon is this blue sphere

I am a fallen angel because I fell from the heaven to down here

I know images can be far beyond what they appear

I know I am an angel but I wonder is this also something known to my peers

I was unbecoming an angel leading myself into destruction a path of doom

I would always say the words I Quit but then I would resume my journey down a path of destruction and doom

A path of doom holds the same consequence as if u were suicidal

It is like I am becoming brainwashed by the oath I chose within the duration of my life cycle

I remember I once guided people who were confused as they gladly awaited my arrival

Now they look to me as a figure that is idle

This is because I am living my life in trifle

I am still confused to who I am and my title

ROLE PLAY 2

I forced myself to re-learn information from my existence; I opened up the bible

Reviewing the files I retrieved from that man I met in that dim-lit room and through all my entire experience

I began to become convinced that the god I served was a man who controlled all mystery action horror drama and suspense

It's like a role play

Like he ponders hmmmm... what character should I portray today?

Which costume should I put on today?

Should I put on the horns and be worshipped by they

or should I put on the black robe on judgment day and judge those who betray

I guess these people don't know the true image of their god until the day their flesh decay

Numerous times I read genesis but there was something I missed

As I read between the lines I gained more knowledge

At age 26 I then took classes in 3rd and 4th grade English

I reflected my learning's from 3rd and 4th grade English and applied them to genesis

Hmmm.... It says create man in our likeness

The words our is plural

So there must have been more than just me amongst many species of mortals

Likeness would mean I possess the capabilities of becoming omnipotent

I possess a brain which gives me the intellect and not mere instinct like animals and rodents

I went from change rich

to brain rich

I know why I was sent here

I was sent here to experience and to enjoy life but take life serious

How would I tell others about something if I never went through something?

To teach in this life I will have to be put in different positions to become included

I will sincerely be able to use the words "I know what you are feeling because I have been through it"

Some people go through life space by space

ROLE PLAY 2

For some the intent was meant for them to indent

No matter how many spaces you skip

you will eventually have to fill in the blanks when you come back to it

Role play:

It's the ability to direct and act your script

Role play;

Through the many positions you play your character will determine the audiences u attract

You will also realize life is one big stage act

There can be drama, action, suspense, mystery, horror, drama, and sorrow

Who knows what the adventure will hold tomorrow?

Role Play;

Chance

Chance

It is what makes us advance

We see the stairs, we can take the steps or we can save the last dance

What does the decision hold?

We already know the answer in advance

We want to see our entire future when we glance

but we can't see everything in advance

I am going to tell a story to u

This story may or may not change your perspective or view

Sit back and watch in 3rd person view

A year after I graduated in 2002 I had an experience of an adult

This experience is brand new

I had a child when I actually didn't mean to

I went from perfect grades to causing havoc on these streets of rage

I didn't understand why things were speeding up at that age

I seen everything within 365 days from crack to death to aids

murder to violence to drug raids

Through all the horrors I was sometimes a spectator or an actor on stage

I have been arrested in the cage

It seems as if I experienced a century of hell in less than a decade

I was a honor roll student with perfect attendance and good grades

What did I do to deserve all this rage...???

Chance

Little did I know a path was being paved

All of a sudden things switched like a trade

People started surrounding me who were a lot older in age from all colors; white to beige

I seen how they lived life through hanging with them I began to experience how they lived life

I have seen it and I have lived it

It's like day-sha- voo I went through it twice in separate lights.

One is where u are in the limelight; u are the participant where the focus and attention is on u

One is where u are the spectator the one who is not a part of the action but watches everything in their view

Now it's review

Through everything u learned u must remember

U must go back to your past and once again become a member

You can't change what happened in the past but u can be a rule-bender

What u been through is a necessary occasion

Take the variables you have learned from your problems and plug them into the equation

What u thought that couldn't be solved was an illusion

And u shall see that when u draw conclusions

When u have the answers which are your solutions the word I can't clogs the mind like pollution

Chance

I seen a lot of action horror drama but I was not on the set; I viewed things from a different take

If I see horror before my eyes I refuse to spectate

I got away and I separated

I seen critics which are people who speculate and end up in a situation that leaves them in bad shape

I would not conversate until I was asked to relate

It's funny how the same scenes u have seen u are now the director u play the role as "the in-between"

I would not intervene if they offered or needed advice I offered them a shoulder to which their heads can lean

Damn!!!

I done this before

It's like I am not an actor on that stage floor

I am learning and teaching like my elders did to me before

One night I came home to a horrible scene and caught my ex-lover cheating and I wanted to scream

It's funny how I was once a cheater also known as a sex fiend

Now I am on the other side, the spectator of the scene

I was strapped with my gun and it had red beams

I am surprised after seeing what I have seen my barrel had no steam

I just told her to gather her things and leave

She put on her clothes and left with ease

For not shooting her god blessed me like a sneeze

I had something to live for that was greater

I learned from the past from people who told me that I never should make a decision that I would pay for later

Chance

I am very thankful that they told me this and they were effective communicators

I would have been in prison missing the green acres

I always wanted more finances

This would cost me to give up the love of my life and I didn't want to take those chances

It was until I was in the comedy stage of my life and she got frantic and pulled a stage antic

She took my daughter without my consent and moved to New Jersey

She did this because she told me to have me she did not feel that she was worthy

At that point, there was the birth of a new me

I had money to buy new clothes and jewelry

I asked for a chance and even though it happened rudely the decision in my favor was a beauty

Sometimes we hate the load that comes with the duty

Even though I felt that she screwed me

Moving along I learned from my last love and in between I had my flings

even though I know now it was not worth a "tic" in my time frames...

But the information I have learned from those scenes within my brain it still sustains

I went back through revolving loops going back to those flings which I call one time-scoops

I did this because I had to get solutions

Solution is proof

I stored this knowledge in my roof for future use

On January 2010 I was suffering from love loss again

I had to take another chance

This chance was to continue to carry emotional baggage or explore new life and take a chance on crossing over to new borders

I felt like a surfer in still-calm waters

Once again I put my heart on the line again so I can regain my spine

Chance

I once thought my heart was the most important organ of mine

I can keep going on and on and on with this story of mine,

But that's chance. It defines things in the future to which we are presently blind...

When U see a tape without a label u will have to insert, fast forward, pause rewind eject etc. and then move onto the next picture in line

U will then have to tell a person what u have seen

With what u have seen u will then have to tell them the theme

U may have to get a roll of film and be a part of those motion pictures even if it means comedy or happiness or horror and blisters

U may have to go back and direct those same motion pictures and show people why there are hot summers and cold winters

You may have to re-visit that production center and be able to tell them why the lighting and the cameras are in the center

Chance makes u fearless while training u to become an expert

If someone asks u about something u will be able to give an answer in more than one sentence; more than an excerpt

Chance is decision making without regards to commerce

It's a choice between hunger and thirst

There may be hurt or a lava-outburst

These decisions are for the better of worst

It's about placement;

Doing what is best for u...

because u come first

Chance

"Chance"

LIFE IS A GAMBLE...PROBABILITY MAY OR MAY NOT FALL IN YOUR FAVOR...

The Glitch

Phase One: Ctrl Key

Control, control, control.

All my life I have been controlled by others

All my life I have been controlled by the desires and wishes of others

This control satisfied them but it has lead me to suffer

We all have traits of family through heredity

When you become an adult it is up to u to continue the legacy

Don't be CONTROLLED by these traits

Do what is in your will regardless of love or hate

Satisfying YOU will feel great

People want to do this. People want me to do that

People want me to become this. People want me to become that

You can make their control fiction or fact

Only you can truly control how u act

It may mean to remove a program from your list of contacts

When u **RUN** your own program you control your own acts

Keep your focus in tact

Haters are viruses with a tremendous impact

If u let their control get to u it can make your screen black

You will see nothing at all because your focus was not in tact

INSTALL an anti-virus that has a life time contract

This anti-virus is a program known as focus

With **FOCUS** u will not feel hopeless

FOCUS creates persistence and positivity and it will detect all **MAL-WARE**

MAL-WARE is negativity

Positivity sparks your brain also known as **MEMORY**

U need **MEMORY** to come up with new creativity

Remove friends from your vicinity

A friend is known as **SPYWARE**

They watch you only to destroy you

To others control don't become a victim

Remove others' control from your **OPERATING SYSTEM**

U are the OPERATING SYSTEM

Don't become controlled and become a victim to another's thought system

Life is typical

U need only one peripheral

U need a **MONITOR** to view

Insight will help get you through

Without these special eyes you will be blind to your environment

THE GLITCH

Environment is an element of surprise

Too many material things also known as **SOFTWARE** will back-up your **HARDWARE**

When it is time to move onto other realms your memory will be overwhelmed and you will get too attached to the material things and lose control of what counts...

YOUR MAINFRAME!!!

Software is necessary to obtain because software expands and exposes the brain

With anothers' control u will not be able to aim

Don't be controlled by others demands

U are the control build your own list of commands

Control is deep

It can rule worlds both shallow and steep

You can control +alt+ delete

You can choose to shut down

If you choose that option heaven will not be a touchdown

There is no heaven for people who choose to put themselves six feet underground

If u choose to shut down u just said "I QUIT" and for you there will be no reboot

U took out yourself it wasn't your calling

U chose your own destiny; u are not god's recruit

When you are under control there are numerous ways to recoup

U will just have to use your memory in your roof

PROMPT yourself to lead to the truth

Control is deep

It can rule worlds both shallow and beyond deep

U can control alt delete and choose to reboot and put yourself to sleep

Not sleep as in death

sleep as in dreaming where u still sustain your breath

These dreams can become true if u bring them into view

THE GLITCH

There are an elite few that can make dreams come true

As these mental stages accrue, u will see a spectrum of your own hue

There are very, very, very few who possess a color on the color spectrum that is brand new

This color is not a mixture of colors to create a color; this color is of a different hue

Not everyone possess the ability to reboot and start brand new

CONTROL yourself don't let others brand you

Phase two: Space Bar - Enter

Space is what separates

It leads us to discover a new face

Space is what separates us apart

U are a portrait unlike no other; you are an original work of art

Don't be afraid to space and divide yourself

if you feel you are getting BE SIDE YOURSELF

If you don't belong there do not enter

Enter only when you are building a new line:

a new paragraph in L.I.F.E.

Enter and space is an abyss that is beyond deep

U can endlessly build sentences on new sheets

It makes what is written make sense; it makes destiny complete

Phase three: DELETE

DELETE erases

DELETE adds new spaces

DELETE adds new characters "persons" things and places

DELETE is secretive it hides what was once in view

It leads u to think there was once nothing there it also can destroy EDIT and UNDO

It is the key that can lead u to the past and the vast

It can change what is written

It can make u GOODRIDDENS

It can change one letter

This one letter can make a sentence confusing or better

Delete can alter or completely change a word and make what was written look absurd

Delete can erase a verb, an adjective, or a noun and other forms of language and communication even pronouns

Delete can be pro-found

Delete can make what was written seem as if it is never to be found

Delete can erase what was written and give birth to a new round

This back space can change inevitability

It also gives the ability for people to build new phrases

These new phrases build sentences

These sentences gives birth to a new paragraph

Delete is the ability to delete the past and make way for a future...

This future is fertility

Phase four: ALT KEY

Alt is an alternative

It is the choices of a list of prompts and commands

It is the choice to get or go against the program

It is a key known as no jam; a choice is given to every woman and man

Without choice there is no land; no grounds for command

Alternative must be manned; it cannot be banned

Phase five: SHIFT KEY

Shift changes the outlook

It also changes our perspective on **INPUT** in our response to **OUTPUT**

ALL CAPS can change how we perceive apps.

U and I may not have the same maps

if I Capitalize, EMPHASIZE, emphasize, ImPrOvIsE e-t-c-

These determine angle, depth, and how we perceive things in three-D

THE GLITCH

Some people hit the escape key

When they can't accept reality

This is like jumping out the window

That is an exit that is very simple

Destiny is etched with a pencil

U can use the opposite end of this utensil

Escape

Your life is not your life to take

THE GLITCH

A glitch is doing something not according to the program

U can prompt, alter, change, and add your own commands

If u carry on a trait passed down by a family a glitch means to be that choice not to continue that legacy

It is building your own blood; doing what is in your D-N-A

Only you can protect u from your environment; u are the E-P-A

Be a glitch

Don't be a stitch which is patching up something from old skin that itch

A bad legacy is contagious

If a bad legacy is not ended it can become contagious and outrageous

Use what was given to all of us

It's the greatest of all inventions

If this is discovered u can control your own intentions

The Glitch= Unknown Key

Fourth Quarter

In the first quarter u have no one in your corner and very few supporters

Your dream is in the making

U have not scored a point on the scoreboard

Once u stop being a loser u will recognize people u have never seen before

These people can be a true supporter

These people can be people who just suddenly enter your life which is your stadium during the final stages because they know success lies in the fourth quarter

When success is in the making

no one wants to play a part in your dreams until your dreams awaken

FOURTH QUARTER

When your dreams awaken and start paying

that's when u will see people who assume a position and start playing

When u let the wrong crowd of people play in your work of creation

u will see some of these people on your same team commit personal fouls

Know that the opposition is not the only people who commit flagrant and technical fouls

During life there will be referees;

not regulators but people who put restrictions and false calls

In the fourth quarter during those winning minutes u will have many supporters;

Some of these attendants will claim to be your descendants

It's very funny how during a dream in those opening minutes

very few if there are a few will desire to be in its attendance

Now when a dream is complete everybody wants a trophy when they never have been a contributor to its finish

These are the very same people who did not see victory during its opening minutes

There will be a dream team

Not dream team as in extra-ordinary or flawless

but dream team as in a league of people who will assist u when they begin to see beneficial causes

A true supporter should be a supporter of your talent regardless

During the fourth quarter of your life as mention once again

in the duration of those final minutes is when u will accumulate attention

People all of a sudden support u because u are winning

U will see an audience of people who never supported you in the beginning

All of a sudden everybody wants to play a position

They want to play a position called the centers of attention

blocking your goals and take credit for everything that you do or mention

FOURTH QUARTER

It's a form of GOALTENDING!!!

Recognize!!

your dream is your dream from the beginning

The talent u possess is god-given

Automated audiences should be forbidden

because they only cheer for u when you are winning

THE FOURTH QUARTER

CENTS

"Sight, smell, touch taste, listen

It pays to pay attention"

Chapter One: A Rude Awakening

Where am I? I can't see.

I lost my sight what has happened to me?

What am I eating...Ice cream.

I can't taste.

Everything I eat lacks taste.

It's like I am eating paste.

I kept saying I was going to quit, but my statements were not legit.

All I did was sniff, sniff, sniff...

My environment is odorless.

All I want is to smell some fresh air.

My environment is odorless when I take a wiff.

I am in a noisy environment. I can hear.

Due to a slight case of paralysis I can't feel my ears.

What happened to my natural gifts?

I am living, but I fell as if I am in an abyss.

This is a state of hell not a state of bliss.

I hear a hiss. What is this...?

I wish I just had one eye,

so I can answer the question where am I.

Chapter 2: Don't Take it for granted

I am walking in a grocery store shopping for chocolate chip ice cream.

I can't seem to find the ice cream.

I approached the store associate and asked" Where's the ice cream"?

"Aisle number nineteen. There's a sign in bright GREEN" Cashier

"Why can't people pay attention all he had to do was use his vision." Cashier *(whispered)?*

What did you say that's not professional.

Whatever!! I got the ice cream went to the register...$4.99?

"Yeah didn't u read the sign?" Cashier

"What are you, color blind...?" Cashier

Excuse me. I didn't see what it says. 4.99

"Well if u READ the BRIGHT YELLOW tag the sale ended on 4/9." Cashier

It's only 11:59pm. The date is 4/8 not 4/9

"Sir your clock is an hour behind we are now on daylight savings time." Cashier

Oh I didn't know. I am sorry how much is it... $4.99...?

"Yes $4.99. Didn't u HEAR me the first time!" Cashier

Excuuuuuse me well here is $5.00!

Keep the penny Ms RUUUDENESS by the way that penny is a TIP for your ruuudeness.

CENTS

“Well here is a nickel. Maybe these 5 cents will remind u to use your 5 SENSES. You know *sight, smell, touch, feel, heeear."* Cashier

“Yeah well u must have thought it was winter to be buying things so cold. By the way is that snow hanging out your nose?” Cashier

No it’s just tissue it’s....j-ju-just my sinuses bothering me u know by it being springtime and all

”Awww! I am sorry to hear that SNOWBALL. “Cashier (while laughing)”

Why is your staff so rude?

Damn Indian bastards!

“It’s just funny to me how u Americans can pay attention to TV, Video games, Porn, and You Tube, but when it comes to using what counts your sight and hearing you all don’t pay attention“ Cashier

“You all don’t think before you ask things. You should research and find things out some things are in front of you and these things are so plain to SEE. “Cashier

“So quick to ask questions and open your mouth...you lack focus.” Cashier

I don’t have to argue with you asshole. I am outta’ here!!

There is no man on earth in the stratosphere and in the entire universe I fear!!

I shop here all the time.

By the way Ms. rudeness why do u wear the same colors all the time?

Are u color Blind?

Bet u didn’t know I recognized that did u now?

I always pay attention to evverythhhING!!!

“You Americans only pay attention to what counts when you can put people down or insult them.” Cashier

“Take your damn items and get outta here! Don’t come back. Before you go, god has given me a vision... **(chanting)** and my intuition tells me he tells you to wake up. Use your natural gifts and pay attention.” Cashier

Get off my hands. you can touch my money but don’t touch me lady!

“God is going to curse you.“Cashier *(while spitting on the customers money)*

What the hell are you going to do, curse my money? It’s already cursed...money is the root of all evil...but I love these paper devils.

"By not believing in him u are going to suffer a rude awakening." Cashier

Yeah okay yea—and you tell who ever that god is of yours that when that wakeup call comes I will just roll over and hit the snooze button haha...what are you god's personal alarm clock, ok *MS CASIO...*

"Sarcastic bastard my name is CASSIE. Can't u read!! My name tag says CASSIE!!" Cashier

Ok Cassie. I said it correctly you happy?

(Exits the store)

Chapter Three: On The Way Home

(Driving in the car)

What the hell was wrong with that cashier?

I mean I know I seen the sign that says frozen goods, but how would I know I can find it there? I know I should have paid attention, but I don't care.

Besides, if I ask for an item it is their job to tell and show me where.

It is not my job to wander around looking around the store and guess where.

I don't even know why those aisle markers are there.

Aww crap! blue lights...

What am I getting pulled over for? I just want to go home and eat some ice cream and enjoy a movie on my nice 60 inch screen.

"License and registration." Ofc. Lancaster

Sure

"Do u know what I stopped u for?" Ofc. Lancaster

What that Indian bitch pressed charges for that argument at the convenience store?

"STEP OUT the car. Shut off your engine." Ofc. Lancaster

I shut off my engine.

I hate guidance and authority and being told what to do especially from officers that are women

primarily because they make decisions and arrests when they are emotionally driven.

"Freeze if you make one move it will be yellow ribbons" Ofc. Lancaster

"Take your hands out of your pockets" Ofc. Lancaster

"Why are your hands hidden? " Ofc. Lancaster

My hands are cold from this freezing cold ice cream my fingertips are froze.

Besides I can't feel my face officer. Don't u see my bright skin and my red nose?

"Sir are u on drugs. Have u been drinking. it is 85 degrees." Ofc. Lancaster

"How did your fingers freeze in 85 degrees? " Ofc. Lancaster

"What is that white pasty substance coming from your nose? I know that is not allergies. For officer safety you are being temporarily detained. Turn around please." Ofc. Lancaster

"I stopped you because u were doing a 100 in a 45. " Ofc. Lancaster

Backseat of the patrol car

I been sitting here for about 30 minutes. Am I going to jail? Here she comes I wonder what she has to tell me. She has a nice shape. I am just fantasizing, hoping she pulls me out the car and nails me.

"Ok I am not going to charge you, because of that suspicious white substance dried out your nose I am going to have to drug test you." Ofc. Lancaster"

Ok no problem officer.

Damn I am thinking to myself, hoping that glue is out of my system. I've been sniffing all day.

I don't want to go to jail. No way!!!

"Ok your results came back ok."Ofc. Lancaster

"I am going to cite you. Then u free to go. By the way, have a nice day." Ofc. Lancaster

I asked the officer can I get a break. I mean damn! I get a ticket. GREAT! *(Sarcastically)*

I bet my chocolate chip ice cream is now melted...Great! My ice cream looks like white paste.

"No u can't get a break. Legally I can arrest you for this. you were doing triple digits in a 45mph speed zone."Ofc. Lancaster

Well officer, I mean *back-off-officer* I'm going to take that ticket and rip it.

The Miranda Rights

I took a pencil and wrote write to remain silent. She told me I have to write to remain silent so I obeyed her wishes and wrote on the ticket paper WRITE TO REMAIN SILENT. I am not being funny I'm just doing as I told *right*.

"Ok smart ass I will put it another way. You are under arrest" Ofc. Lancaster

"You are being charged with reckless driving, and disorderly conduct "Ofc. Lancaster

What is the charge? How much is that $4.99.

"Ok pal you are way out of line" Ofc. Lancaster

County Jail

Never been here before. I can't sleep well in places I never been before.

I can't get comfortable. This bed feels like a concrete floor.

When I sleep in odd places I have odd dreams.

Some of these odd dreams are so real that they feel as if they are going to manifest in real-life scenes.

Chapter Four: Odd Dreams in Cell block fifteen

(Sleeping) Zzzzzzzzzzzzzz'sss

Black circles...Venom...Snakes...Tongue...Pinocchio...nose gets smaller and smaller...

ZZZZZZZZZZZZ"SSS

(Gasps and awakes)

HUH!!!

What the hell was that about?

The following day the judge let me out on signature bond since I have never been in trouble before.

Man I have a terrible headache.

Ever since I been in jail, I can't SEE or THINK straight.

What is going on? I have an excruciating headache.

I can't SEA OR THINK straight.

Chapter Five: Revisitation

I looked in the yellow page directory and I came across an eye care place.

Man! I got such a terrible headache I have to get my eyes checked.

OPTOMETRIST EYE EXAM

"Sir we have checked your vision and according to your previous visits your eyes were perfect. Have you been reading in the dark?" Optometrist

No. I just had a bad dream.

"Are you sure you didn't have any eye injuries." Optometrist

No. I just had a bad dream.

"Ooh sure you did. "Optometrist

Why? What seems to be the problem?

"It seems you are suffering more than a stigmatism. You are going blind. We don't quite understand what greatly affected your sight at this time, what we need from you is your recent activities. Are u able to recall and rewind?" Optometrist

No. All I did was have a bad dream!!

I got frustrated and left the doctor's office and I still can't sea.

What is he talking about?

Man! My head hurts.

I will just take some headache medicine that should help.

Convenience grocery store

I went to get some more chocolate chip ice cream. After visiting the eye-team I went in the store and I didn't see the cashier on the sales floor.

Hmmm... Did that mean she is off today?

I seen another clerk on the sales floor and asked about Cassie.

CENTS

"You shouldn't be so nosy. Are u related to her?" Store Manager

No. I was just wondering...

"Umm... Have you been sniffing paste?" Store Manager

Wh-Whhat?

"Well I see white residue of the substance on your face. Lately, we been having high theft here." Store Manger

" I have been watching the camera. You visit the stationery aisle quite often. Do you do artwork, you always buy paste." Store Manager

Nnno I mean... *(Sigh)*

I just do carpentry...you know like carpenter in house work. I am remodeling my home I live alone. I have tremendous work to do on my own.

"You mean, you get high at home." Store Manager

No, the fumes just get to me that is why my head hurts. I just came to get some ice cream

Ok I will see you later. you know me I am a regular customer.

"HEY!! You have to pay for that." Store Manager

I didn't know. It says BYE get one free. I have stigmatism I can't *sea.*

"No, it says BUY ONE GET ONE FREE. Not bye as in walk out with it" Store Manager

I am sorry I am serious I can't sea I have a vision problem I am not being funny

"Well, if u can't see then you need to not shop here anymore. READING is essential before purchasing. Pay attention!" Store Manager

Damn! You are just as rude as your employee, that cashier of yours.

"Well, she works another job." Store Manager

"She works at Palmolive. It is right up the street. You should talk to her. She can tell you a lot about destiny. She guides us around here. She has an amazing gift. You should visit her sometime." Store Manager

I DON'T NEED TO VISIT HER!

I can see my future. I need no one to tell me about my destiny.

I need no one to tell me to do anything. I have my own guidance.

I led myself in the *write* path thus far, so I need no help.

Here's $4.99. GOODBYE!

Chapter Six: Five Minus Two

I was at home, miserable as usual and I couldn't focus without my inhalant glue.

I couldn't FEEL anything. I couldn't get high.

DAMN!

My ice cream tasted good. My hands got a little numb. Maybe it is the coldness that numbs my hands.

It took me an hour to get 7 scoops from a pint. My vision is blurry and I can't *sea.*

I couldn't aim my spoon in the *write* place. Besides, I could feel my face but it seems I was losing my TOUCH...

Maybe it's the ice cream. It is cold and all...

I have to find some new drug to get me high.

I can't feel the high from this glue at all.

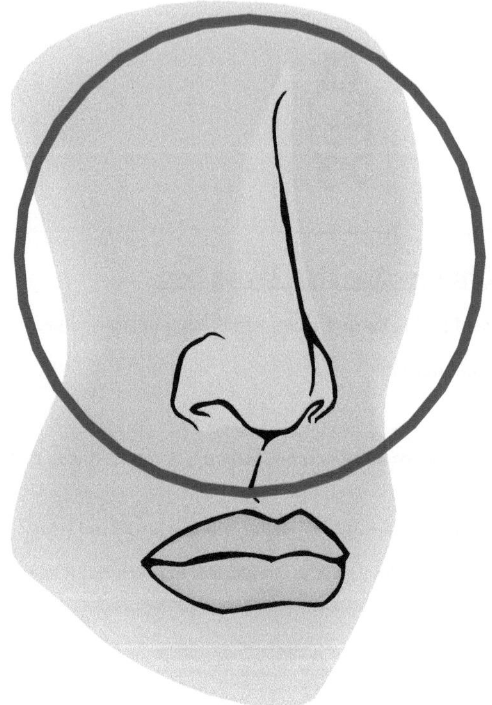

The Nose

Chapter Seven: 5 minus Three

I have trouble *seaing.*

I have to *sea* my friend IAN.

He has some coke. Maybe that feeling will give me a high of some hope.

"Damn u look stoned dude. What do you need. "Ian

I need some cocaine. This glue isn't enough.

CENTS

"Well here u go. I got some more supply for a lower price. If times get tough come and see me sometime." IAN

Yeah, well I will come and *sea* you sometime.

"Ok man."IAN

I went up the hall and went back to my room. I inhaled the glue fumes, sniffed 2 lines off a straight spoon.

After an hour, I still didn't FEEL a buzz.

I proceeded to go down the hall. I saw IAN being taken out in handcuffs by the fuzz.

DAMN!! No more drugs he's busted.

Then it hit me. I finally felt a buzz.

It felt so good, then after FIVE minutes or so it went away.

I am having trouble with my *site,* my touch, and my smell.

I can't even tell what I am smelling when I inhale.

I looked on the floor and seen a slithering snake.

I turned my head once again because I had to do double take.

AHHHHHH!!!!

SNAKE!!!!

The rattle snake bit me then slithered under the door at a fast rate.

I wondered why I couldn't feel my face.

It's the venom numbing me.

I then dialed 911. I hope I am still alive when they come for me.

Chapter Eight: Hospital

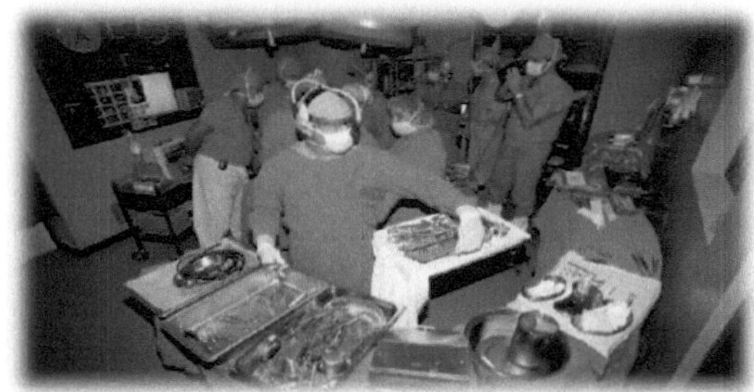

EKG machine *(Beep, Beep, Beep, Beep)*

"Sir can you hear me. Can you see me. Can you feel when I test your reflexes. Can you..." Dr. Fleming

Yes I hear you.

"Well it seems you have not been bitten by a snake. We discovered cocaine but no venom in your system." Dr. Fleming

Wh-What you gotta be kidding. That can't be right. I have seen it. I felt the sharp stinging bite.

"Well the police say they shot the snake and the snake didn't bite you. They say a mysterious woman was seen walking down the hall." Dr. Fleming

Who was she?

"She was Esha Cassie Turner; an Indian woman. She lives in apt. 312, 4 doors down from yours 316... She just moved in about 2 weeks ago. She heard you screaming and she notified the police for you" Dr. Fleming

"She saved your life even though we have found not one snake bite. "Dr. Fleming

What?? Cassie, that's the cashier at... She works... Ok I am ready to discharge out the hospital now since there is nothing wrong with me.

"Do you believe in god? "Dr. Fleming

Uuughhh!

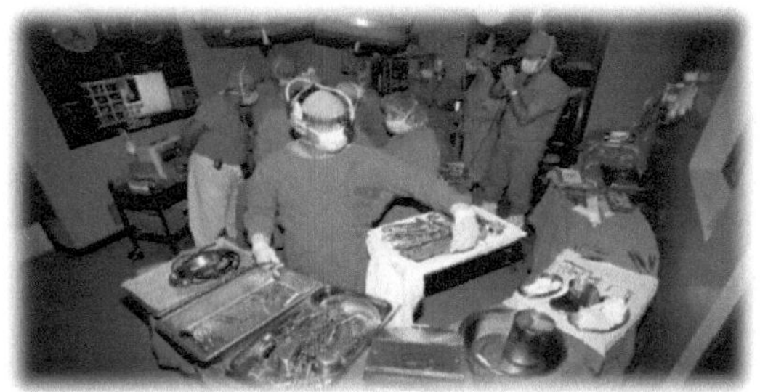

"Well that remark makes it very clear of your beliefs. You see god works in mysterious ways and we have no idea and no medical explanation to why you are losing some of your five senses " Dr. Flemming

"You shouldn't take anything in this life for granted, even if it is automatically given to you. " Dr. Fleming

"You need to connect with him." Dr. Flemming

Yeah. Ummm... I will. Can I go now...?

"Sure. Here are your discharge papers. Our procedure is that you leave by wheelchair " Dr. Flemming

(escorted out the hospital)

Chapter Nine Palm-O-Live

What is going on with me?

I thought this was a dishwashing factory, but it was a palm reader's place.

WAIT!!!

That cashier I got rude with really was psychic.

"Hello. We meet again" Cassie

Yeah I guess.

"Well why have you come here." Cassie

I can't *sea.* I am losing my *site.* I can't *sea.* My *tuch* and my *smale.* I am confused

"What do you believe in?" Cassie

I am aetheos. I don't believe in god.

"Well do you now?" Cassie

Not quite, but can you really tell the future?

"To an extent." Cassie

"Close your eyes. Give me your palms." Cassie

Ok. *(closes eyes)*

"Aah. uh huh. oh no!" Cassie

"Ooo... I love how this feels" Cassie

What did u see? What's wrong?

"Get as far away from me as you can." Cassie

"My god has a command for me." Cassie

"It's my time to SEE reality." Cassie

"If I don't do what I was told with my gift of intuition: my 6th sense: My natural gift will be taken from me like it was taken from you." Cassie

What do you m-m-mean?

“Well you have taken advantage of your natural gifts, your five senses, and because u didn't use them in the right manner they were taken from you. He, God has sent you warning signs. Didn't you see them?“ Cassie

No.

“Did you have dreams?“ Cassie

Yes.

“Well all the things you have seen in those odd dreams has come true.“ Cassie

“The Pinocchio nose getting smaller and smaller means you are losing your sense of smell” Cassie

“You sniffed cocaine, glue, you did all the wrong things with the gifts that were naturally given to you.“Cassie

U see the snake the venom symbolized loss of your FEELING your touch but in reality GOD has not lost feeling for you” Cassie”

“I have seen the snake. When it ran away beside my door apt.316.“ Cassie

What about the dark circles?

“The dark circles represent your eyes. You have gone color blind and because you were blind to reality then you don't need your eyes.“ Cassie

“You soon will be fully blind if you don't use what was given to you naturally.“ Cassie

“There are deaf children who want to hear. There are people who want to see that are blind. There are people who are deaf and blind who pay attention more than people with all of their senses. Listen and hear. Observe and view. Taste and enjoy. Smell and analyze. Feel and touch. People are so quick to speak, but lack using their mind.“ Cassie

Forget you!!!

Was he there when my little brother got killed? Was he there for me when my wife left me?

Was he there-*(interrupted)*

“Stop stop stop!!! You will lose this battle if you continue.“ Cassie

“You don't run the show. You are just another guest appearance in my god's venue. He gives you control of your performance and thus far you have performed very poorly within your life “Cassie

What kind of god is, this sacrifice...?

I sacrifice things every day. So what's the problem?

CENTS

I do th-th-th-th- that I ca-ca- can't sp-sp-sp-sp-speak what's that symbol of the ni-ni-ni- nickel for?

"5 cents represents 5 senses. It also means...? *(clears throat)* you should go now." Cassie

What does it mean? Wait! in my dream... I seen all the signs except a nickel.

Why is the picture of a nickel here?

Wait! Weren't you colorblind?

You are wearing blue today. You know like I told you in the beginning, I always pay attention. I think u sacrificed your vision for my vision. Your touch for my touch and such and such

You misused your senses. You used your intuition and your 6th sense to gain my fifth sense.

You saved my life because u needed a live sacrifice.

A dead person wouldn't serve a purpose.

"You are not leaving out of here until I get what I want." Cassie

"I want to see again I miss seeing the colors! You don't use your eyes or your nose for any good uses." Cassie

"You use your nose for substance abuse. Why should you need those senses? " Cassie

The rattle snake bit me on my leg. I can't feel my leg.

I can't see, but I swiftly reached for the snakes head.

I felt a slimy texture.

I heard a hiss near my ear.

CENTS

I know I grabbed the head of the snake in the right position, according to the distance adjacent to my ear.

The rattle on the tail was far away. I heard the hiss close to my head.

I heard Cassie talking, so I quickly approached the sound of her voice.

My arms reached out and my sense of touch helped me.

I felt lips and I knew it was her mouth.

I swiftly shoved the snake in Cassie's mouth.

I heard a scream from her and at that point I knew the venom from the snake injected in her mouth when she and the snake went mouth to mouth.

When I didn't hear her shout I knew she was dead.

I heard a hiss from the snake.

Even though I know I didn't have my sight, my sense of touch became enhanced.

For some odd reason I can predict when the snake advanced.

I didn't have the sense of sight with pure eyes but I grabbed a knife nearby.

I cut off the snake's head.

I didn't hear a hiss or a rattle. I knew then the snake was dead.

I took my arms while I was groping around and with my sense of touch I tripped over

someone's foot.

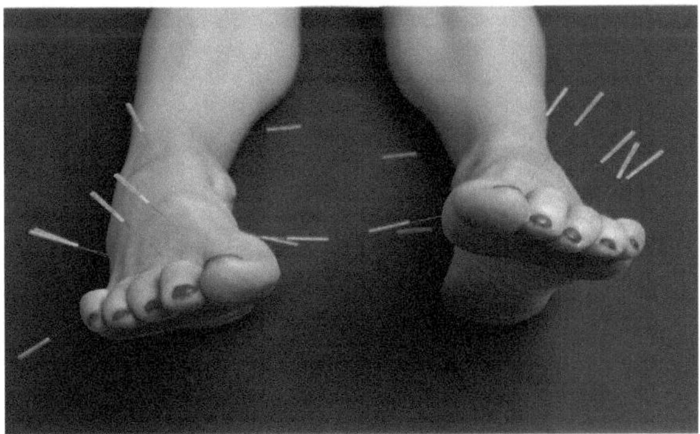

It must have been Cassie's heel.

While I was crawling on the ground I continued to grope around.

CENTS

Went from Cassie's toe to her head

and I chopped off her head to ensure she was dead.

It's like her curse was reversed.

I seen everything within my mind.

My senses began to incline.

It's like a cinema of events passed through my mind from her mind.

I then knew her sense of intuition became mine.

I may barely be able to see but the ultimate eye was within me.

I may barely feel but my sense of emotion regained slowly as Cassie's curse heals.

I may barely be able to smell, but I can still sense something is bad, good, new, or stale.

I may have lost some of my naturals, but with the sense of intuition I can't fail.

My senses became advanced as they rapidly heightened to a greater scale.

CENTS

I played back these cinemas with Cassie's intuition and prediction senses and everything she touched was upon me.

I realized she was stripping my senses from me.

She tricked me into thinking god was taking all of these things from me. All along It was her doing this

I wonder is god a myth...?

I know the answer to that now that I ***know*** my god really does exist.

Cassie was colorblind.

Cassie thought it was right to use her god given gift in which I now possess through psychic inheritance.

She used it to punish those who took things for GRANTED...But she misused it...

It wasn't to be used in that nature.

I know I will never see or smell again,

but with this 6th sense intuition clairvoyance I see things on both ends.

I wish I appreciated my natural gifts and was not amongst ungrateful men.

For me a new sense of reality begins...

CENTS

I am not sad. I grin because I was given an opportunity to see him for who he really is once again...

My god is more than my god; my god is my friend and he is also my kin.

"Cents"

Morality:

PRESENTS in the PRESENT can later lose its PRESENCE; if u do not cherish its ESSENCE.

CENTS

The placement of words can change the perception of the perspective observed

OBSERVE!!

PRESENTS in the Present can later lose its PRESENCE... if u don't cherish its ESSENCE

^

Can ESSENCE later lose its PRESENCE if u don't cherish its PRESENTS?

^

ESSENCE can lose its PRESENCE if u don't cherish its PRESENTS...

^

PRESENCE can later lose its PRESENTS if u don't cherish its ESSENCE...

"For every point of view

There is a subconscious point of view

There are other perspectives too

Which aspect(s) applies to you?

Can u create a new?"

"Cents"

Resistance

U know, one day we will all have to let things go

As for me, I have never been a person to disregard information offered by my elders

I look to them as helpers

U see, one day we will all assume their position

even though we all may not make it to see that grey-haired transition

Being an elder is not age

An elder is a mental state

Experience, knowledge, learning and applying information from our mistakes is great

For example in the year 2010 on august fifth

I tried to explain to a woman the meaning a word called gift

Not gift as in presents

RESISTANCE

Gift as in presence

U see, it is a gift to have someone in your presence

Company is an element of mankind's essence

On the other hand, I am aware
that some of the information that we offer to share
is too much for some of our mind's to bear

As for me materialization and worldly things is of little concern and care

and at the age of 26 this is a condition that is very rare

I am fine as long as I have my talents, my music, the clothes i wear

and a moment of peace along with a breath of fresh air

You can't dwell on anything in this world

It comes it disappears
and never reappears

If u become too dependent on what was there

u will not be able to move on from there

Learn, experience, shed tears

Enjoy the remaining segments of your life and leave the rest in the rear

Enjoy it while it is here

and keep the memories up there

When it comes to change, some people display fear

They do not want to shift they want to remain in 1st gear

and expect everything to automatically transition from there

Life itself is a manual transmission

It is up to us to shift, change, and hit the clutch

Some of us get stuck in a habit or old rut

and wonder why the gears to our lives begin to rust

Primarily, it is because u were scared to change and level-up

and give your life a tune up

It should not take for us to lose something completely to realize you need to let it go

RESISTANCE

It is no longer physical it does not exist no more

For instance, I never quite understood why it takes for something physical to undergo an absence from existence

for us to consider it absence on our attendance

Maybe it's resistance

U must let go of what sparks a state of dependence

in order to exercise independence

As long as we know something physically exists

our desire will always be to touch it with our fingertips and clench it with our fists

Some people grip on to their past to the extent it begins to rip and tear

Through all the technology we have invented and discovered

the realm of death is still uncovered

Just think if man was able to intercept death

he will not be willing to let go any physical object

Let Go!!!

RESISTANCE

What's old

Let it mold

Don't fear changes be bold

Switch the program don't reload

May your destiny unfold

It shouldn't take for something to completely disappear

For u to state the words "It ends here"

If it takes for an object to physically disappear
for u to let go of what was there

Then your idea of letting it go was not sincere...

Resistance....

Heroin

Today Is August 8th 2010:
And as always I am in a deep state of mind once again.
I just got off the phone with a friend.
He opened up my mind to the concept of how women are similar to
the drug heroin.
A woman by nature is an emotional creature.
I learned from experience which is my best teacher.
No matter their lifestyle if they are rich, poor, middle-class, high class with daily earnings comparable to the annual salaries of teachers
women are materialistic as they judge things according to its actions, smell and features.
For an example, when u gain INTEREST in a woman when u first meet them
the judgment begins upon when u first greet them
There are select things that a woman won't try when u first meet her.
She knows nothing about you so there are certain things she won't try until the relationship gets deeper.
On the other side when I mention the statement of "showing INTEREST" I mean interest as in percent.
If u don't have nothing to "chip in" or present
then they will turn away from anything that does not represent "a beneficial intent".
If a woman can manipulate man's frame of mind
which is known as man's design
she will see you as a keeper.
If you are a "true architect"
And you know the blueprint to a woman's intellect
you will be the one she rejects
simply because u know her like a book's index.
She will turn her back on you like Brutus did Caesar
and runaway like a race that measures 100 meters.
It's all because u know how to read her.
Finders Keeper.
Women are heat-seekers.
It's the thrill
in a conflict of interest with the chill.
When you touch smell and feel
or when you use the words "I am hot as hell"
the truth of these words will reveal
when u show a woman too much passion and devotion
which are categorized as extreme emotions
man will lose his intellect and he gains emotion.
Man then begins to react off of mere emotion
and enters into this state of mind where all thought is stolen.
Similar to an animal such as wolverine also known as Logan,
you will be known as the X-Man
within the category of the Ex-men
who refused to supply and give in.
What is E-Motion...???
Emotion is energy flowing like the water that is freely flowing.
Why do u think women are in tune with the moon, and the currents in the ocean...?
Finders' keeper;
as I have previously stated in the beginning of this poem and u would have grasped the concept by now if u were an "in-depth in between the lines reader".

HEROIN

Similar to how snakes see things in infrared vision
"How hot" something seems is the basis of a woman's decision.
Snakes and women both are creatures that are emotionally driven;
like Adam and Eve and the tree that was forbidden.
Even through the storm a man must maintain his mental position and do not give in.
Even the bible supports the worst thing is a woman's scorn.
Upon them when it is wrong you perform
a woman will then be out for blood and evil just like the children of the corn.
Women are creatures of e-motion
Just like the currents flowing
and the tides rising in a chaotic ocean.
On the flipside, is it such a CO-INCIDENCE when it comes to the term "you got me open".
Similar to something that is padlocked
and unlocked
what a man has is "The key".
Not key as in gaining access to a keyhole within a doorknob's handle.
I mean key as in a piano.
It's the mere sound
that gains access to their hearts which I call a beat and pound.
On the other side, a man can be
something as physical as a key
if a woman has emotional baggage and a man possess' that combination key
to let their luggage free depending upon a woman's perception degree.
Not degree as point of view or angle.
I am talking about degree, as in temperature heat and fire.
How this goes is according to if u acquire
that code or G-code(game) that unleashes a woman's padlocked desire(s).
Women are comparable to drugs.
A man will see that once he falls in love.
Everything goes according to what the man does.
If you do anything dirty all it takes is ONE footprint in the mud
and a woman will forever hold that grudge
against u for taking them through the sludge.
At that point things will never be like it was.
A woman will then play games and begin to test you
and say "Baby I wish u were like when I first met u".
Similar to a high,
time after time they will try.
Nothing will ever be comparable to that first high.
A woman will then begin to search for that other guy
if you don't have the product(s) to maintain her high.
If you are that heroin
then u will always maintain her from here on in.
HEROIN....
The addiction begins...

HEROIN

When a man continuously permits a woman's desire for material(s) there will be an infinite desire of supply and demand.
Things will then begin to get out of hand.
At this point a man has to continue to supply material things known as products and the addiction will never end.
HEROIN...
Once u give a person their ultimate high
their desire for more and more will never die.
They WANT, and WANT, more and more getting caught up in the things that are physical and they start to become unspiritual.
Some women will begin to look at material things as if it were a ritual.
This is what happens when u overdose an individual.
U supplied them with the highest product and the ultimate high
There will be no high that is identical.

Heroin...

Replay

(Dayshavoo or Rendezvous…?)

I am in the year 2010, but I am living like I was in 1994

It seems as if I have been here and done this before

Have I...?

I am not quite sure

I have day-sha-voo- upon every corner I tour

I am in an abyss, but courage forces me to explore

As I learn more information

from my current situation

I then rewind back to my past, without the use of teleportation

Is this my designation...?

Or is this my destination...?

Within these different positions

within these different dimensions

I still see the same visions

Am I in these positions because of my own decisions..?

No matter the transition, I still see repitition

I was them, I was he, I was you and every pronoun in-between there too

I once was the tailor, the seller, and the wearer, of your shoe and the positions in-between there too

The environment that encompasses you is a clue...

We all have checkpoints in which we must rendezvous(ron-day-voo)

It is visitation

then revisitation

REPLAY

Through visitation,

we learn information

Through re-visitation, the mind goes into a state of transformation

We then take this information go back to the same location and begin to use methods of application

What is the purpose of information without application...?

L.I.F.E. is prime factorization

There are many forms of civilization

Reality serves u with realization...

L.I.F.E. is not a prime...L.I.F.E. is **prime factorization**

L.I.F.E. (Learning Information From Existence)

/ \

L.I.F.E. (Learning Information From Experience)

/ \

L.I.F.E. (Learning Information From Experimentation)

/ \

L.I.F.E. (Learning Information From Exploration)

/ \

L.I.F.E. (Learning Information From Example)

/ \

L.I.F.E. (Learning Information From Environment)

/ \

L.I.F.E. (Learning Information From Expiration)

/ \

L.I.F.E. (Learning Information From Emotions)

??????Many More?????????? It is infinite.....?

L.I.F.E. (Learning Information For Eternity)

REPLAY

L>I<F>E=Learning information From Existence

DYE

Do we die...?
or do we dye...?
there are various perspectives to which they are invisible to the human eye
A structure,
is just an appearance based upon a wavelength of color
The soul and spirit are components necessary to the physical infrastructure
Light,
is what reveals and unreveals objects upon our sight
Without light,
we will not see how dim or how bright
When one's spirit and soul loses its physical
the skin's spectrum become invisible
The soul or spirit are neccessary components to one's physical infrastructure
Without soul, or spirit there would not be a physical structure
Physical is just a mirror;
the spirit is the pallbearer
Everything you earn
will have to be placed in an urn
The desires for these solid manifestations are destined to burn;
from its chemical sense what have you learned...?
the experience is something to which u should be concerned
Dye reflects pigmentation in reference to the intensity of its signal strength
Light has pigmentations of many wavelengths
We don't DIE...
We DYE...
We are on a higher spectrum invisible to the naked eye
At my funeral, there is no need to cry;
i dont want to see condensation in your eye
I want to see smiles,
As I DYE....

DYE

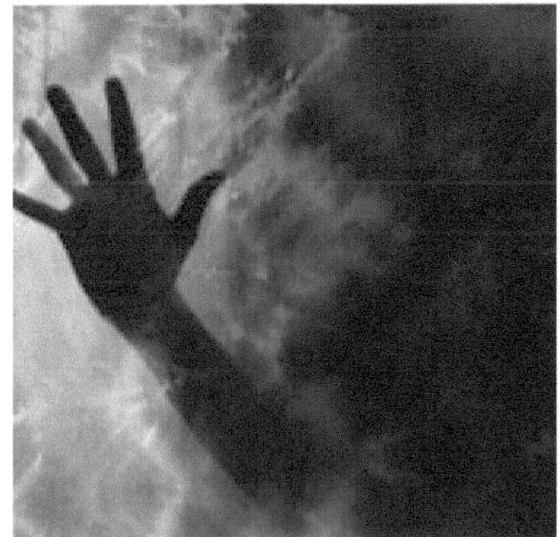

Is it die…?

Or do we DYE…?

L.I.F.E. IS LEARNING INFORMATION FROM EXISTENCE

U MUST FIRST EXIST IN ITS REALM...

BEFORE U BEGIN TO EXPERIENCE

IF U TAKE LIFE SERIOUS;

L.I.F.E. THEN BECOMES

LEARNING INFORMATION FROM EXPERIENCE

I can see the L.I.T.E.

GO THROUGH THE L.I.T.E.

L.I.T.E. (Learning **I**nformation **F**rom **E**xperience**)**

Welcome to the other aspect(s) L.I.F.E.

TREE OF L.I.F.E. AND COMMUNICATIONS

L.I.F.E. is a maze

It is puzzling; These are some parts of the constructs of the maze

What is L.I.F.E.

Learning **I**nformation **F**rom **E**xistence

^

Learning **I**nformation **F**rom **E**xperience

^

Learning **I**nformation **F**rom **E**nvironment(you have your **E**ncounters and **E**xamples**)**

^

Learning **I**nformation **F**rom **E**xploration(conscious levels: higher= **E**levation and lower= **E**xcavation)

^

Learning **I**nformation **F**rom **E**xperimentation(you have your **E**xercises, **E**xhibits, **E**xplanations**)**

^

Learning **I**nformation **F**rom **E**motions

^

Learning **I**nformation **F**rom **E**xpiration(Information constantly changes and so does life)

^

Learning **I**nformation **F**rom **E**volution(old brings in the new and reverse this process too)

?

?

?

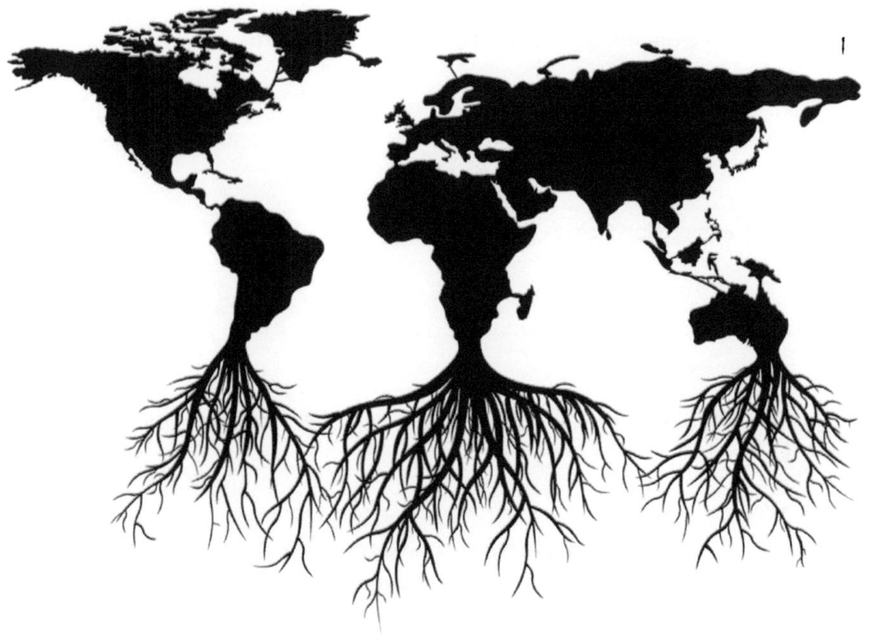

L.I.F.E. is an education process

"I gave you the tree

Now I want the future roots...

to give these branches fruits...

and finish and confirm its solidity"

Closing Arguments

These views are not my emotions.

This is not philosophy (feel-osophy)

These are not my views; this is more than photography

This is reality…

All of these experiences have happened to you

I know to experience this it will be like déjà-vu (Day-sha-voo)

U will go through this over and over again and that is a fact

Life has no end

Therefore, you are the pen. You create the punctuation. You have a control over your destiny to a certain extent and degree. You are the inventor and discovery of your journey.

You create, and discover the laws which make you an exotic attorney

Everyone has a fatality**(fate**-ality)

The Directors Cut

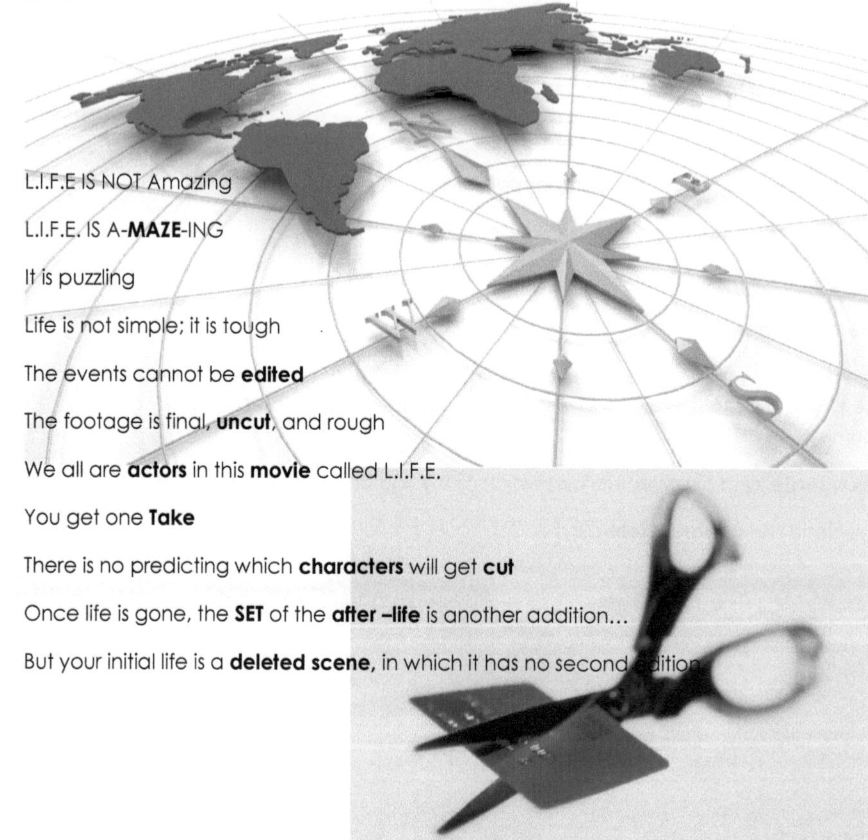

L.I.F.E IS NOT Amazing

L.I.F.E. IS A-**MAZE**-ING

It is puzzling

Life is not simple; it is tough

The events cannot be **edited**

The footage is final, **uncut**, and rough

We all are **actors** in this **movie** called L.I.F.E.

You get one **Take**

There is no predicting which **characters** will get **cut**

Once life is gone, the **SET** of the **after –life** is another addition…

But your initial life is a **deleted scene,** in which it has no second edition

CREDITS

L.I.F.E. is = **L**earning **I**nformation **F**rom **E**xistence

U must first, **EXIST** before you begin to experience

L.I.F.E. then becomes **L.I.F.E. =**

Learning **I**nformation **F**rom **E**xperience…

If you take your encounters serious

L.I.T.E. = **L**earning **I**nformation **T**hrough **E**xperience

Camera = Learn by Witnessing It

Action = Learn by living It

CREDITS

R.A.I.D. UNIT ENTERTAINMENT

888 315 7324

twitter.com/therealeskay

facebook.com/raidunit

twitter.com/cashklay

raidunit@gmail.com